Original title:
In the Stillness

Copyright © 2024 Swan Charm
All rights reserved.

Author: Kätriin Kaldaru
ISBN HARDBACK: 978-9916-89-802-4
ISBN PAPERBACK: 978-9916-89-803-1
ISBN EBOOK: 978-9916-89-804-8

Unraveled Thoughts in Sacred Silence

In the hush of prayerful night,
Whispers float on wings of light.
Hearts entwined in quiet grace,
Seek His presence, a warm embrace.

In shadows deep, where spirits dwell,
The sacred truths begin to swell.
Voices lifted, soft yet clear,
A promise held, we need not fear.

With every breath, a seed of faith,
Nurtured deep, life's sacred wraith.
In solitude, divine abide,
In tangled thoughts, the soul confides.

Through trials faced, we find our way,
In silence, He invites us to stay.
A gentle hand that leads us forth,
To untangle what we seek in worth.

So in the stillness, hope is found,
Each thread of love, a sacred sound.
In unraveled thoughts, we see the sign,
In sacred silence, His light will shine.

Ascent into the Sacred Quiet

In silence deep the spirit soars,
Finding peace on heaven's shores.
Each whisper brings a gentle light,
Guiding us through sacred night.

Tranquil hearts in prayer unite,
Embracing love, dispelling fright.
In every breath, a holy sigh,
As we ascend, our souls reply.

Hymns of the Softened Spirit

Softly sung, the echoes rise,
Carried on the wind to skies.
In melodies of grace we find,
The soothing balm for troubled mind.

Each note a prayer, each chord a plea,
Binding hearts in unity.
Let the hymns of love resound,
In the sacred space we've found.

A Breath Between the Worlds

In the stillness, moments blend,
Where time begins and loves extend.
A whispered breath, a fleeting thought,
Connecting realms, peace wrought.

With every heartbeat, life unfolds,
A mystery that love beholds.
In the space where souls converge,
The sacred breath, our hearts emerge.

Reflections in Sacred Stillness

In quiet pools, the spirit sees,
Reflections dancing on the breeze.
In every glance, a truth revealed,
In sacred stillness, hearts are healed.

The mirror shows our inner light,
Illuminating darkest night.
With every wave, our doubts released,
In tranquil waters, souls find peace.

Stars Above in Sacred Stillness

Stars twinkle softly in the night,
Whispers of hope in the celestial light.
Silent prayers rise like smoke,
In the embrace of the heavens bespoke.

Each star a promise, gently bestowed,
Guiding the weary along the road.
In the stillness, hearts find peace,
From worldly troubles, sweet release.

Layers of darkness cradle the glow,
Reminders of love that continuously flow.
The vastness above, a divine embrace,
Inviting the soul to seek its grace.

Quietude of the Heart's Belief

In the quietude, faith softly sings,
Echoing trust in all life brings.
Amidst the chaos, calm takes hold,
In whispered prayers, truths unfold.

The heart beats slowly, attuned and clear,
To the gentle voice of love drawing near.
Patience blooms in silent waits,
Opening wide the heavenly gates.

Belief is a garden, nurtured with care,
In solitude's presence, we learn to share.
Every moment, a blessing we see,
In the quiet, our spirits fly free.

Faithfulness Found in Silence

In silence resides a steadfast heart,
Faithful and true, never to part.
Words unspoken, yet deeply felt,
In quiet resolve, our spirits melt.

Each pause a journey, profound and deep,
In the stillness, our souls softly leap.
Listening closely, divine voices call,
In the sacred silence, we find it all.

When the world shouts, we choose to be still,
Finding our power in the strength of will.
Faithfulness grows in moments concealed,
In the temple of silence, true bonds revealed.

The Beauty of God's Hidden Moments

In the shadows, beauty does play,
In hidden moments, light finds its way.
With each heartbeat, a miracle stirs,
In the depths of silence, hope occurs.

Nature whispers secrets, soft and sweet,
In the rustling leaves, the divine we meet.
A glimpse of grace in a fleeting glance,
Life's treasures unfold, a sacred dance.

The unseen touches our hearts each day,
In the gentle breeze, God's love will sway.
Cherish these moments, softly bestowed,
In the beauty of silence, our spirits are flowed.

Whispers of the Sacred Silence

In silence, faith takes flight,
Gentle breezes hear our plight.
The stillness holds divine embrace,
In twilight's glow, we find His grace.

Each heartbeat sings a sacred song,
Where souls unite, we all belong.
In moments hushed, we glimpse the truth,
The whispers guide, the heart uncouth.

Through shadows deep, the light will seep,
In prayerful pause, our spirits leap.
The sacred whispers soothe the night,
In every breath, we find His light.

Beneath the Veil of Quietude

Beneath the veil, where angels tread,
In tranquil hearts, the Spirit led.
Celestial peace, a soft embrace,
In quietude, we seek His face.

A whisper flows like gentle streams,
Where hope is born and love redeems.
In every sigh, we find our way,
As blessings wash our fears away.

Through stillness, wisdom's voice prevails,
In sacred light, the truth unveils.
With open souls, we find our place,
Beneath the veil, in His embrace.

Echoes of the Divine Embrace

In echoes soft, the heavens call,
A symphony that fills us all.
Each note resounds, a sacred rhyme,
In spirit's dance, we touch the divine.

The whispers flow like gentle tides,
In every heart, the love abides.
Beyond the dawn, the shadows fade,
As hope arises, unafraid.

With open arms, we seek the grace,
In every breath, His warm embrace.
The echoes of love light up the space,
In unity, our faith we trace.

Serenity in the Seraphim's Gaze

In seraphim's gaze, tranquility reigns,
With every whisper, peace sustains.
Through ethereal light, our spirits soar,
In sacred stillness, we crave more.

The heart knows not of doubt or fear,
In harmony, the soul draws near.
With wings of faith, we rise above,
In every dawn, the light of love.

The silence sings with sacred grace,
Within the depths, we find our place.
In seraphim's gaze, forever stay,
Embraced by love, we find our way.

The Holy Presence in Gathered Silence

In silence deep, we humbly stand,
The Spirit's breath, a guiding hand.
With hearts aligned, we seek the grace,
In sacred stillness, find Your face.

Each whispered prayer, a lantern bright,
Illuminates the veil of night.
Together bound, in love we dwell,
The holy presence speaks so well.

In gathering light, our souls unite,
The softest touch, a pure delight.
In every moment, we embrace,
The wondrous peace of this safe space.

As echoes fade, a quiet sound,
We feel the joy that's all around.
In gathered hearts, we find our song,
The sacred space where we belong.

With faith as strong as mountain peaks,
We hear the truth that silence speaks.
In holy reverence, we arise,
To witness love that never dies.

Embracing the Solitude of Faith

In solitude, the spirit grows,
In quiet realms where solace flows.
With every breath, I seek Your call,
In whispered prayer, I give my all.

The world outside may roar and chase,
But in this stillness, I find grace.
The heart is tuned to sacred ways,
In gentle light, my spirit stays.

Oh, solitude, my trusted friend,
In Your embrace, my fears shall end.
With every moment, truth unfolds,
A sanctuary that love beholds.

Deep in my soul, Your presence reigns,
As shadows fade, no more the chains.
In faith's embrace, I rise anew,
A journey guided straight to You.

The stillness holds a sacred space,
Where doubt dissolves, and hope takes place.
With open heart, I walk this path,
In solitude, I find Your wrath.

A Stillness Filled with Divine Promises

In quiet dawn, the promise gleams,
A stillness filled with holy dreams.
With every breath, a hope anew,
In whispered words, I turn to You.

The morning light begins to break,
Each gentle wave of grace I take.
In tranquil hearts, Your love will bloom,
A chorus whispers, dispelling gloom.

Where silence reigns, Your spirit pours,
Through crafted stillness, hear our scores.
In deep reflection, truth awakes,
A bond that nothing can forsake.

In every moment, each sweet sigh,
Divine assurance fills the sky.
In faith's embrace, we shall not roam,
For in Your arms, we find our home.

With every promise, hope ignites,
In the soft glow of holy lights.
Together bound, our spirits rise,
A dance of love that never dies.

The Heart's Whisper in Sacred Quietude

In sacred quiet, whispers flow,
The heart reveals what we should know.
With gentle beats, the truth aligns,
In stillness deep, Your love defines.

The sacred hush, a guiding star,
Each moment spent feels never far.
In silence, trust finds roots so deep,
The heart awakens from its sleep.

In quietude, the soul takes flight,
A melody of pure delight.
With every pulse, Your grace draws near,
A sacred bond, forever dear.

Soft echoes of a holy song,
Invite us all to join along.
In this communion, all is clear,
The heart's true whisper calms our fear.

With every yearning, love transcends,
In sacred silence, time suspends.
Together bound in holy light,
Our hearts proclaim the love so bright.

Reverent Moments of Quietude

In stillness, hearts do find,
A sacred whisper in the mind,
The gentle breath of dawn's embrace,
A moment still, a holy space.

The world beyond, a distant call,
Here in silence, we stand tall,
With every thought, we seek the light,
Guided by the peace of night.

Each breath a prayer, each sigh a plea,
Awash in grace, we yearn to be,
In reverence, time begins to bend,
A quiet moment without end.

The shadows dance, the candles glow,
In this calm, our spirits flow,
Holding fast to the truth we find,
In reverent moments intertwined.

Through faith, our burdens gently lift,
In these moments, a sacred gift,
Together we rise, with hearts anew,
In quietude, we journey through.

The Prayer of Unspoken Time

In the hush where silence reigns,
A prayer lingers, free from chains,
Unspoken words, like softest sighs,
Reach the heavens, touch the skies.

Time becomes a sacred thread,
Woven gently, quietly spread,
We gather hopes in whispered tunes,
Touched by light of silver moons.

The soul's deep yearnings softly wake,
In this space, our spirits break,
Grounded firm in the morning dew,
We stand united, brave and true.

Each silent plea, a bridge we build,
In sacred moments, our hearts are filled,
With trust in what we cannot see,
The unseen hand, our guide will be.

Through every still and passing hour,
We seek the grace, the hidden power,
In this prayer, our souls align,
In unspoken time, we intertwine.

Meditations Beneath the Quiet Sky

Underneath the vast expanse,
We find our hearts in tranquil dance,
With every star, a story glows,
In silent peace, the spirit grows.

The moonlight spills a silver hue,
Kissing earth with drops of dew,
In meditations soft and deep,
We hold the world, our souls to keep.

Each thought a feather, light and free,
Drifting through the endless sea,
Of dreams and hopes that lift us high,
Beneath the vast, embracing sky.

As whispers of the night unfold,
Ancient truths, in silence told,
With every breath, we close our eyes,
To touch the peace that never dies.

In quiet moments, we discern,
The fires of faith forever burn,
Together, here, we shall abide,
In calm reflections, side by side.

Shadows of Tranquil Devotion

In shadows cast by flick'ring flame,
We whisper peace, we speak Your name,
In tranquil nights, our spirits soar,
Devotion held forevermore.

Each heartbeat echoes, soft and clear,
A melody we long to hear,
In the quiet, grace descends,
Our hearts awakened, as love mends.

With every breath, we weave a prayer,
A tapestry of hope and care,
The light of faith, our guiding star,
In shadows deep, we know You are.

Through trials faced, we rise anew,
In tranquil devotion, bond held true,
Together, we walk this sacred path,
In every moment, love's sweet wrath.

With open hearts, we seek to know,
The depths of grace, the spirit's flow,
In shadows cast, our souls unite,
In tranquil devotion, purest light.

Surrendering to the Sacred Whisper

In shadows deep, I seek the light,
A gentle voice, a guiding sight.
With heart laid bare, I bow in prayer,
Embracing grace within the night.

In silence, whispers softly call,
A tranquil peace, I heed the thrall.
Each moment still, my spirit grows,
To trust in love, surrender all.

As branches sway in sacred breeze,
The heart finds solace, sweet release.
In every breath, a chance to feel,
The presence of the soul's own peace.

Awake, arise, the dawn anew,
In every breath, the sacred drew.
With open heart, and spirit free,
I journey on, to depths so true.

Surrendering to the soft embrace,
A dance of faith, in sacred space.
With every step, in humble trust,
I find my home, my holy place.

Blessings Found in the Hushed Morn

The morning breaks, a soft-lit hue,
In every ray, a promise true.
The world awakes, each doubt subsides,
As blessings bloom where skies are blue.

In whispers low, the heart can hear,
The sacred songs that draw us near.
With each new light, and every sigh,
A tapestry of love appears.

The dew-kissed grass, the still of dawn,
In gentle grace, the fears are gone.
A moment rare, where time stands still,
A sacred breath, each burden drawn.

As sunlight warms the quiet ground,
In every corner, peace is found.
In gratitude, the heart will sing,
For blessings shared, and love unbound.

So rise and greet the day with bliss,
In every breath, a sacred kiss.
For in the hush, the heart will know,
The love that flows, the light we miss.

The Gentle Call of Sacred Reflection

In stillness found, the soul takes flight,
A call to pause, in soft twilight.
The mirror deep, reflects the truth,
In sacred calm, our hearts ignite.

With every breath, the silence grows,
A whispered prayer, the spirit knows.
In gentle waves, the mind can clear,
As light descends, the soul bestows.

The heart, a canvas, sacred space,
Invites the light to interlace.
In every thought, a chance to heal,
The gentle touch of love and grace.

As rivers flow, we find our path,
In stillness, laughter blends with math.
A sacred dance, where shadows play,
The heart awakens from the wrath.

Reflecting deep, the spirit shines,
In quietude, the love aligns.
In every moment, find the peace,
The gentle call, where spirit twines.

A Sanctuary Built in Silence

In quiet realms, the spirit grows,
A sanctuary, where compassion flows.
With every pause, the heart finds rest,
In sacred stillness, love bestows.

The walls of silence, strong and wide,
Embrace the weary, hearts confide.
In whispered prayers, our dreams take flight,
A sacred place where hopes abide.

Each breath a hymn, each thought a prayer,
In silence wrapped, the world laid bare.
With every moment, know the grace,
That fills the void, the love we share.

So build your faith with bricks of peace,
Let silence reign, let anger cease.
In every pause, a chance to grow,
A heart reborn, a sweet release.

In this sanctuary, souls unite,
In sacred bonds, love shines so bright.
With open hearts, and voices low,
Together, we embrace the light.

The Sacred Pause of Creation's Breath

In the hush of dawn's embrace,
Creation whispers soft and low,
Stars align in tranquil grace,
A sacred pause, the heart will know.

From silence blooms a vibrant light,
In stillness, worlds begin to spin,
Awake, the spirit's pure delight,
In sacred space, all life within.

Nature sings a gentle hymn,
Each breath a note within the song,
In the still, the edges slim,
Of time, where all the souls belong.

Embrace the now, let worries cease,
In fleeting moments, find your truth,
In quiet arms, discover peace,
In every heartbeat, wisdom's youth.

Beneath the arch of heaven's dome,
The secrets of the heart unfurl,
In creation's breath, we find our home,
A tapestry of love, a pearl.

Stillness Beckons the Soul's Journey

In the quiet, whispers call,
Inviting us to rest and see,
The sacred space where shadows fall,
Stillness beckons, setting free.

Steps of faith on paths unknown,
Each moment holds a sacred light,
In the silence, seeds are sown,
Guiding souls through day and night.

Learn to dance with gentle grace,
To feel the pulse of time unfold,
In every breath, a soft embrace,
The journey cherished, stories told.

Listen deep, the spirit sighs,
In stillness flows the river wide,
With open hearts, as love replies,
We walk together, side by side.

In quietude, find solace rare,
Each heartbeat paints a tale divine,
The soul's journey, a prayer spare,
In the stillness, all align.

Moments of Grace Amidst the Silence

In the pause between the notes,
Moments woven, grace arrives,
In the quiet, wisdom floats,
The spirit dances, truth survives.

Softly falls the morning dew,
Whispered blessings on the ground,
In silence, find what's pure and true,
And in stillness, love is found.

When voices fade and echoes wane,
The heart attunes to deeper sound,
In moments pure, release the pain,
For in silence, joy is crowned.

With open arms, the spirit sings,
Each breath a gift from realms above,
In silence rests the sacred wings,
Where every heart can learn to love.

Hold the stillness in your care,
In every moment, breathe the grace,
For in this hush, a light we share,
A fleeting glimpse of heaven's face.

Illuminated Paths of Silent Watchfulness

The twilight sparks with sacred glow,
In watchful silence, we remain,
Paths illuminated, breath to flow,
Hearts are tethered by love's refrain.

Each step, a whisper, soft and clear,
In the stillness, purpose shines,
Within the calm, our fears we steer,
In watchfulness, the soul aligns.

Like stars that guard the night so deep,
Each moment holds a gleaming thread,
In silent keep, our secrets seep,
Where hope ignites, and fear has fled.

With every heartbeat, shadows fade,
Illuminated by grace's hand,
In watching still, the light cascades,
A journey charted, bold and grand.

Together in this quiet place,
The spirit wanders, free and bright,
In silent watch, we find our grace,
On paths of love, we find the light.

The Echo of His Love in Silence

In quiet woods where shadows dwell,
The heart finds peace, a sacred well.
His love resounds, a gentle breeze,
A whisper heard among the trees.

Each silent prayer that leaves the soul,
In stillness vast, we feel made whole.
The echoes linger, soft and true,
In every sigh, I feel Him too.

With every dawn that breaks the night,
His presence glows, a guiding light.
In solitude, my spirit sings,
Awash in grace, the hope He brings.

Here joy abounds in fleeting hours,
Where silence blooms like fragrant flowers.
In love's embrace, I find the way,
To walk in faith, each blessed day.

Celestial Whispers Beneath the Stars

Beneath the canopy of night,
The heavens shine, so pure, so bright.
Each star a prayer, a message sent,
In cosmic love, my heart is bent.

The moonlight paints a silver path,
To linger here is love's sweet bath.
In whispers soft, the cosmos speaks,
A truth divine, in silence seeks.

With every twinkle, every gleam,
A promise wraps me in His dream.
In starlit skies, my soul finds rest,
With faith, I know I am truly blessed.

The galaxies in chorus hum,
A sacred tune, forever sung.
In every heartbeat, love abides,
As nature swells, and peace resides.

Whispers of the Silent Heart

Within the depths where stillness grows,
A quiet heart, the spirit knows.
In whispers soft from deep inside,
His gentle love, my constant guide.

The silence speaks in sacred tone,
In solitude, I am not alone.
Each thought a prayer that rises high,
As love renews and fears comply.

With every beat, my heart relates,
To boundless grace that never waits.
In humble truths, I lay my fears,
He hears my heart, He dries my tears.

In moments shared with quiet grace,
I find my strength in love's embrace.
With faith unshaken, I shall stand,
In silent trust, held in His hand.

Sacred Echoes of Solitude

In solitude, the spirit roams,
To find the source of holy tomes.
Each echo sings of love divine,
A tranquil heart, in peace, aligns.

The world outside may fade away,
Yet in this stillness, I shall stay.
Across the fields where silence flows,
His gentle voice within me grows.

In sacred moments, truth unfolds,
With whispers soft, the heart beholds.
In every sigh, a prayer ascends,
To God who loves and never bends.

The quietude, my soul's embrace,
In longing hearts, I find His grace.
To listen deep, to love's sweet call,
In solitude, I find my all.

Finding Grace in Gentle Shadows

In the quiet dusk of day,
Whispers of peace softly play.
Hearts lifted in tender prayer,
Finding grace in the still air.

Soft light dances on the ground,
In every heart, love is found.
Moments paused in sacred bliss,
In gentle shadows, we find His kiss.

The trees sway with sweet refrain,
Nature sings of love's great gain.
Each leaf rustles, a hymn so true,
In shadows, our souls are renewed.

The stars awaken in the night,
Guiding travelers with their light.
A gentle hand leads us home,
In these shadows, we are not alone.

Through every trial, faith will rise,
In hidden places, He replies.
With every heartbeat, hope draws near,
In gentle shadows, we persevere.

When Time Surrenders to Solitude

When silence blankets the land,
In solitude, we understand.
Each tick resounds, a sacred beat,
In the stillness, we find our seat.

Moments stretch beyond the stars,
Time whispers of healing scars.
In the quiet, His presence glows,
A sanctuary where worship flows.

As the world fades from our sight,
Hearts awaken in the night.
In solitude, a spirit glides,
In the calm, our faith abides.

Still waters reflect the divine,
In this hush, our souls align.
In prayer, our burdens release,
When time surrenders, we find peace.

Embracing silence, voices cease,
In solitude, we find our lease.
Time bows down, yielding its claim,
In this stillness, we learn His name.

The Breath of the Eternal

In the morning's gentle breath,
Life awakens, conquering death.
Every inhale sings of grace,
In the stillness, we find His face.

From the mountains to the sea,
The eternal whispers, 'Come and see.'
In each heartbeat, His love flows,
In the breath of the wind, He shows.

Every breeze carries a prayer,
In the silence, He meets us there.
With each sigh of the grateful heart,
The eternal teaches us to start.

Through each moment, we are blessed,
In His presence, we find rest.
The world fades as we rejoice,
In the breath of the eternal, we find our voice.

Each step taken, a divine dance,
In His mercy, we find our chance.
The rhythm of life, a sacred tune,
In every breath, we greet the moon.

Embracing the Light Within the Quiet

In the stillness, a spark ignites,
A beacon shining through the nights.
In whispered prayers, we embrace,
The light within our sacred space.

Calm waters mirror the divine,
In peace, our souls intertwine.
Every heartbeat echoes bright,
Embracing the light in the night.

The dawn breaks with soft delight,
Illuminating our inner sight.
In every moment, grace pours through,
The light within guides us anew.

As shadows linger, we stand tall,
In His presence, we hear His call.
With open hearts, we learn to trust,
Embracing the light, rise from dust.

In quiet moments, love appears,
Washing away all doubts and fears.
With every breath, we come alive,
In the light within, our spirits thrive.

Meditations on the Holy Pause

In silence we find grace,
Where whispers touch the heart,
Divine presence in stillness,
A sacred time to start.

The echoes of our thoughts,
In reverence we bow down,
Each moment softly speaks,
In faith, we wear the crown.

From chaos to calm seas,
A breath, a gentle sigh,
In the pause, God's embrace,
Heavenly wings do fly.

With each heartbeat mindful,
We gather here in prayer,
The world fades far away,
As we breathe in His care.

So let our spirits rise,
Like incense in the sky,
In the holy pause we dwell,
Where souls cannot deny.

In the Sanctuary of Soft Sounds

In this hallowed space of peace,
Where the soft sounds reside,
We listen to the rustle,
Of angels by our side.

The murmur of the leaves,
A symphony of grace,
Each note a loving whisper,
In this holy place.

The gentle trickle flows,
From the waterfall's embrace,
Nature's hymn surrounds us,
As we seek His face.

With every breath we take,
We feel the presence near,
In the sanctuary of soft,
We hold the holy dear.

Let the quiet embrace,
Transform our weary mind,
In soft sounds, we discover,
Peace that's pure and kind.

Celestial Reflections on a Still Pond

Glistening under moonlight,
The pond holds what is true,
Reflections of our hearts,
In the depths, we pursue.

Stars shimmer in the water,
Whispers from on high,
A dance of light and shadow,
Where earthly spirits lie.

The stillness speaks of blessings,
In ripples, soft and slow,
Each wave a prayer ascending,
To the heavenly glow.

In nature's quiet canvas,
We find our souls unfold,
Celestial reflections,
Of the stories yet told.

With faith, we cast our hopes,
Into the mirrored gleam,
In the still pond, we gather,
To weave our sacred dream.

The Hushed Prayers of the Soul

In the twilight's tender grace,
The soul begins to speak,
With words that don't require,
A voice that feels so weak.

Hushed prayers rise like incense,
Carried on the breeze,
To the heavens above,
With gentle, whispered pleas.

Every heart a temple,
In silence still we stand,
The language of our spirits,
Echoes through the land.

In moments of deep stillness,
We find the light within,
The hushed prayers of our souls,
A journey to begin.

Let our hearts be open,
To hear His soft reply,
In the hushed, our spirits soar,
Touched by the endless sky.

Clarity Found in the Silence of Prayer

In quiet moments, hearts align,
Whispers of hope, softly entwine.
A gentle peace fills the soul,
In silence, we find that we are whole.

Veils of worry, cast aside,
In prayer's embrace, let faith abide.
Every sigh, a sacred plea,
In stillness, we're set free.

Words may falter, but love remains,
The divine answers through our pains.
In the hush of twilight skies,
Truth emerges, and spirit flies.

From depths of doubt, a light ignites,
In sacred space, we find our sights.
The heart, a vessel, pure and bright,
In silence, seek the guiding light.

Through the stillness, clarity calls,
In prayerful moments, the spirit enthralls.
Awakening grace, our souls entwine,
In silence of prayer, we truly shine.

Soft Light Breaking Through the Darkness

As night descends, shadows creep,
Yet hope remains, though we weep.
A promise glows, softly near,
In the stillness, love draws near.

Through stormy paths and weary days,
We seek the light in countless ways.
A flicker shines, in hearts it stays,
Guiding us on through the maze.

With every dawn, a new chance grows,
In darkest times, the spirit knows.
Soft light breaks through, sweet and warm,
In faith's embrace, we find our calm.

The morning calls, a gentle sound,
Through trials vast, our strength is found.
A guiding star, bright and pure,
In the darkness, we endure.

Whispers of dawn through night's cold breath,
Speak of life, and conquer death.
In every glimmer, hope remains,
Soft light of love, through all our pains.

The Graceful Dance of Muffled Voices

In sacred halls, where echoes sway,
Voices rise like a soft ballet.
Muffled songs of prayers shared,
In unity, our hearts are bared.

Each whisper carries truth divine,
In the spaces where spirits shine.
Though spoken low, their power's vast,
In the hush, our souls are cast.

Steps of faith in rhythm flow,
Guided by love, we learn to grow.
In the dance, each breath encapsulates,
The grace of life that reverberates.

Harmony weaves through solemn space,
In every voice, a holy trace.
Together we rise, together we fall,
In muffled tones, we heed the call.

A symphony where silence sings,
Embraces all the joy it brings.
In the grace of this shared refrain,
Muffled voices break the chain.

In the Pause of Eternity

In moments held, the world stands still,
A timeless breath, a gentle thrill.
In the pause, infinity bends,
Where love begins and never ends.

We stand at the edge, hearts collide,
In the quiet, divine resides.
Each heartbeat a whisper of grace,
In eternity's soft embrace.

Time unfolds, a sacred thread,
In the silence, all is said.
Awakening truth, ancient and wise,
In the stillness, our spirit flies.

Each fleeting second, a glimpse of light,
In the pause, all wrongs feel right.
Within our souls, a cosmic dance,
Every heartbeat, a sacred chance.

As we linger in this serene space,
We find our place in love's warm embrace.
In the pause of eternity, we come to see,
The beauty of life, forever free.

The Pilgrimage of Unspoken Praise

In silent steps, we tread the ground,
Seeking grace where love is found.
Each heartbeat whispers sacred hymns,
In shadows cast by life's own limbs.

The path is wrought with trials old,
Yet faith within the heart is bold.
We wander far, yet never stray,
In every breath, a quiet pray.

Mountains rise and oceans gleam,
In every pulse, a hidden dream.
Through valleys deep, the spirit glows,
In every thorn, the blossom grows.

With every step, our burdens light,
In the darkest hour, we find the light.
As we ascend, our souls embrace,
The journey speaks of endless grace.

We gather strength from every song,
In unison, we all belong.
For in this pilgrimage we stand,
Hand in hand, with faith's command.

Resting in Divine Emptiness

In quietude, our spirits sigh,
In emptiness, we learn to fly.
The world falls silent, shadows fade,
In this stillness, love is laid.

We lay our burdens at His feet,
In hollow space, our hearts meet.
Every echo, a whispered prayer,
In the void, we find Him there.

No need for words, just gentle grace,
In the emptiness, we find our place.
The soul unfolds, like petals wide,
In the calm, we abide inside.

As stars above begin to glow,
In His embrace, our fears let go.
Each moment, pure, without the strife,
In this divine, we find our life.

In tranquil peace, we learn to dwell,
In the emptiness, all is well.
For in that void, the heart does see,
The infinite love that sets us free.

Soul's Soliloquy in the Quiet Shadow

In the shadow's gentle fold,
The soul speaks truths, untouched, untold.
A whisper echoes in the night,
In solitude, we seek the light.

Each thought, a prayer left to fly,
In silent dreams, our spirits sigh.
With every breath, the heart unfolds,
In quiet corners, wisdom holds.

The moonlight dances on the ground,
In peace, a harmony is found.
The world outside may roar and spin,
Yet silence sings of peace within.

In solitude, we learn to trust,
In quiet shadows, love is just.
Our spirits soar, our voices blend,
In silent moments, hearts transcend.

For every whisper holds a grace,
In the shadow, we find our place.
The soul's soliloquy rings clear,
In the quiet, God draws near.

Beneath the Clouds of Stillness

Beneath the clouds, in soft embrace,
We find the peace of sacred space.
With gentle winds, our worries cease,
In nature's arms, we taste His peace.

The rustling leaves, a song of grace,
Each moment pregnant with His face.
In every breath, the spirit hums,
In stillness, love eternally comes.

The mountains bow to silent skies,
In quietude, our spirits rise.
With every heartbeat, hope ignites,
Beneath the clouds, our faith invites.

As dawn awakens, colors blend,
In the stillness, hearts ascend.
The quiet calls, we heed its plea,
In tranquil moments, we are free.

For in the hush, we hear His voice,
In stillness, we rejoice, rejoice!
Beneath the clouds, we find our song,
In the arms of love, we all belong.

Peace Within the Divine Embrace

In stillness, hearts find grace,
Where whispers of love interlace.
Guided by a sacred light,
We soar beyond the night.

In every tear, we see the fate,
A gentle hand to participate.
Every breath, a prayer we share,
In the warmth of divine care.

With faith, we rise and stand so tall,
Embracing peace that conquers all.
In shadows, hope ignites the flame,
In unity, we call His name.

The heart beats in a tender hymn,
In love's embrace, we are not dim.
Whispers soft like morning dew,
Reminding us we are made new.

Let every soul find shelter here,
In the grace that draws us near.
With open arms, He welcomes all,
In divine love, we shall not fall.

Chants of Grace in the Silent Night

Beneath the stars, our voices blend,
In harmony, our spirits mend.
The moonlight bathes us in its glow,
A sacred space, where love can flow.

In quietude, we find our strength,
As faith unfolds its blessed length.
Each whisper lingers in the air,
A reminder that we're held in care.

With every note, the heavens sway,
The soul ignites, with hope we pray.
In the stillness, we feel His grace,
A tender touch, a warm embrace.

And in the night, a promise gleams,
Life's tapestry woven with dreams.
In unity, we raise our voice,
In silent night, we rejoice.

Let hearts entwine in the gentle peace,
Where doubts and fears find their release.
With each chant, we draw more near,
In every heart, His love is clear.

Somewhere Between the Breath and the Thought

In breath we find the sacred pause,
A fleeting moment to cause applause.
The space between, where wonders dwell,
In silence, echoes a timeless bell.

With every thought, a prayer ascends,
Where grace abounds and love transcends.
In the stillness, spirits bloom,
Illuminating the darkest room.

Here we dance on sacred ground,
With every heartbeat, love is found.
In whispers soft, we hear His voice,
Guiding us to rejoice in choice.

In this realm, where faith renews,
We walk together, and we choose.
In unity, our souls ignite,
Somewhere between the day and night.

Let gratitude fill each fleeting breath,
In life's embrace, we conquer death.
In this journey, we find our grace,
Between the breath and thought, we trace.

A Reverent Pause in Eternity

In the stillness, time stands still,
A sacred moment, a gentle thrill.
In reverence, our spirits rise,
Gazing deep into the skies.

With every heartbeat, love unfolds,
Stories of grace eternally told.
In this pause, we feel the flow,
Of every dream, of all we know.

Threads of faith weave through our days,
Guiding us in life's intricate maze.
In the quiet, His presence shines,
With every breath, the heart designs.

Let us gather in this embrace,
Flowing gently through sacred space.
With open hearts, we share His light,
In reverent joy, our souls take flight.

Lost in wonder, we humbly stand,
In the love that joins hand in hand.
A pause in time, where we belong,
In eternity's embrace, we are strong.

Reflections of Faith in the Quiet Night

In the hush of the evening light,
Whispers of prayer take their flight.
Stars above, each a guiding sign,
A reminder of love divine.

The moon casts shadows, soft and bright,
Calling hearts to take a moment's plight.
In silence, souls begin to mend,
Finding their way to a sacred end.

Deep breaths draw in the night's cool air,
In stillness, we release our care.
Faith blooms gently in the dark,
Even in doubt, we find a spark.

Each thought a prayer, each sigh a plea,
In this moment, I am free.
With open hands, I seek the light,
And cradle faith throughout the night.

So let us walk this path together,
Through winds of change, and stormy weather.
In every echo, love resounds,
In every heartbeat, grace abounds.

The Sanctuary Within: A Journey in Silence

In quiet corners of my soul,
I find a haven, pure and whole.
A gentle whisper guides my way,
In stillness, I bow down to pray.

The world outside may churn and spin,
But here within, my heart can win.
Each moment wrapped in tender grace,
A sacred bond, a warm embrace.

Beating softly in silent tones,
The sanctuary within me groans.
With every breath, I seek to hear,
The voice of love, so sweet and near.

I journey forth, a steady light,
Embracing whispers of the night.
Where faith and trust have intertwined,
In silence, true peace I find.

As echoes linger, hopes arise,
With open heart, I touch the skies.
Each step I take, a dance of grace,
In silent joy, I find my place.

Serene Embrace of the Divine's Stillness

In the calm where shadows play,
I pause to hear what hearts convey.
The divine breathes in tranquil sighs,
Wrapping love in sacred ties.

Every moment, a cherished gift,
In stillness, my soul begins to lift.
Beneath the stars, I feel the peace,
With faith, my worries find release.

Time stands still in twilight's glow,
In the silence, grace does flow.
Each heartbeat echoes soft and true,
In every breath, I feel renewed.

The world fades to a distant hum,
As whispers of the night become.
With open arms, I feel the peace,
In divine stillness, my heart's at ease.

In this embrace, I find my way,
Guided by love, come what may.
With every prayer, my spirits soar,
In the stillness, I am evermore.

The Pathway of Quiet Blessings

Along the pathway, blessings bloom,
In whispers freed from worldly gloom.
Each step a prayer, each gesture kind,
A journey woven, heart aligned.

In gentle light, the shadows fade,
As quiet blessings softly wade.
With every breath, the spirit dances,
In tranquil moments, love enhances.

The path is lined with hope's embrace,
In silence, I behold His grace.
With humble heart, I seek to share,
The quiet love that lingers there.

In every corner, peace invokes,
A gentle smile, a laughter's stokes.
Together we weave a sacred thread,
On this blessed path, love is spread.

So let us walk this course of light,
In unity, both day and night.
With every step, our spirits rise,
Quiet blessings beneath the skies.

Hear the Heartbeat of Heaven

In the stillness, hear the call,
Waves of grace, they rise and fall.
Whispers echo through the night,
Heaven's rhythm, pure and bright.

Each moment sings a sacred song,
To the faithful, they belong.
Hearts unite in prayer and peace,
In His love, our souls find ease.

The stars above, they dance with glee,
Marking paths of destiny.
Every heartbeat, a divine touch,
In this truth, we find so much.

Feel the promise in the air,
A gentle presence everywhere.
Lift our voices, share the bliss,
In His grace, there lies our kiss.

Together in this sacred space,
All are held in warm embrace.
In the heartbeat, we reside,
In His love, we shall abide.

Bathed in the Soft Glow of Faith

Underneath the twilight glow,
Gentle breezes softly flow.
Faith ignites the darkest night,
Guiding hearts towards the light.

In the calm, our worries cease,
Finding solace, finding peace.
Every prayer, a guiding star,
Leading us from near to far.

Radiance within each soul,
In this warmth, we are made whole.
Bathed in love, we rise above,
Witnessing the grace thereof.

Hands together, strength we share,
In this journey, we declare.
With each step, our spirits soar,
Faith unfolds at Heaven's door.

The dawn brings hope, love's refrain,
In our hearts, we break the chain.
Bathed in faith, together stand,
In His light, we join His hand.

The Sound of Unity in Quietude

In the silence, we are one,
Gathered 'neath the rising sun.
Hearts aligned in sacred tune,
Singing softly, morning's boon.

Voices blend in harmony,
Filling souls with reverie.
Each whisper, sacred and clear,
Ties that bind us, ever near.

In the still, His presence dwells,
Every tale of grace it tells.
As we gather, rich and bold,
Stories of our faith unfold.

The sound of unity resounds,
In our hearts, His love abounds.
Quietude, a prayerful art,
Binding us, soul to heart.

Let us cherish every breath,
Celebrating life, not death.
In the sound, we find our way,
Together in His light's ray.

Silence that Speaks of His Love

Within the silence, whispers play,
Echoes of the love we sway.
In the quiet, truth unveiled,
His sweet promise, never failed.

Softly wrapped in tender grace,
Every heartbeat in its place.
Silence breathes with open arms,
Holding peace, embracing charms.

In the stillness, we can hear,
Every prayer, each hidden tear.
Love surrounds in sacred space,
In His presence, we find grace.

Moments pass, yet He remains,
In our joys and in our pains.
Silence that speaks of His love,
Guiding us, like stars above.

In our hearts, the echoes last,
Binding present with the past.
In the quiet, sweet and whole,
Heaven's song within our soul.

When Divine Presence Lingers

In quiet corners where shadows dance,
The whispers of grace call us to glance.
Each breath a prayer, each sigh a hymn,
In the stillness, our spirits swim.

The light cascades through vaulted skies,
In sacred silence, our hearts arise.
Veils of longing softly unfold,
As stories of mercy are gently told.

In fleeting moments, eternity meets,
Where every heartbeat and truth greets.
A tapestry woven with love and care,
In the presence divine, we lay bare.

Beneath the stars, beneath the sun,
In every heartbeat, we are one.
With souls entwined in a dance so grand,
We find our purpose, hand in hand.

When doubts arise and shadows loom,
We seek the light, dispelling gloom.
For in the presence, all is revealed,
Our spirits uplifted, our wounds healed.

The Sacredness of Moments Unrushed

In the stillness of a morning light,
Each droplet of dew, a diamond bright.
We breathe in peace, our hearts aligned,
In moments unhurried, love designed.

Rushing rivers teach us the way,
To honor each billow, each sway.
The dance of petals in gentle breeze,
Whispering truths that put us at ease.

In stillness, time bends and flows,
A sacred pause, where serenity grows.
We glimpse the divine in each simple act,
In silence profound, hearts interact.

As shadows lengthen and colors blend,
We gather the moments that never end.
With gratitude woven in every thread,
Life unfolds in the path we've tread.

In quiet spaces, we find our grace,
With every heartbeat, a warm embrace.
Savor the present, let worries cease,
In the sacredness, we find our peace.

A Pilgrimage in the Hushed Expanse

On paths less traveled, we roam and seek,
In the hush of nature, the soul can speak.
With every step, a prayer ascends,
In the stillness, our journey bends.

Mountains high and valleys low,
Guide our hearts where the wild winds blow.
Each moment a token, a blessing rare,
In whispers of faith, we breathe the air.

We wander through forests, wise and deep,
Where ancient voices in silence keep.
In shadows and light, the sacred stirs,
In the heart's echo, the spirit purrs.

With each horizon, horizons unfold,
Stories of ages still waiting to be told.
We gather the treasures, unseen and grand,
In the pilgrimage, we take a stand.

Through trials and triumphs, we press on,
In a dance with the dusk, the breaking dawn.
In faith, we trust, as we lift our gaze,
On this sacred journey, our spirits blaze.

Gazing into the Infinite Calm

Beneath the stars of a velvet night,
We find our peace in the soft twilight.
With open hearts, we gaze above,
In the infinite calm, we feel love.

The moonlight bathes our souls in grace,
In whispers of silence, we find our place.
Time seems to pause, as dreams take flight,
In the embrace of the luminous light.

Waves of the ocean, rhythms so sweet,
In their gentle cadence, our spirits meet.
Every wave tells a story of old,
In the calm embrace, we break the mold.

As dawn paints the sky with blush and gold,
We gather the promises the day will hold.
With each sunrise, our hopes renew,
In the infinite calm, we are true.

So let us linger in moments divine,
In the sacred silence, our hearts entwine.
To gaze into forever, eternally blessed,
In the tranquil presence, we find our rest.

The Serenity of Divine Embrace

In stillness found beneath the stars,
The heart soars high where peace resides.
A whisper felt in sacred hours,
A love that in the silence guides.

With open arms, the Spirit waits,
To cradle dreams and mend the soul.
In gentle light, we find our fates,
Together, whole; together, whole.

The journey marked by tender grace,
Each step a prayer, each breath a hymn.
Within the depth of His embrace,
We lose ourselves, and yet grow limb.

The warmth of truth, so pure and bright,
Encircles all who seek His face.
In darkest nights, He gifts His light,
A promise made, a sweet solace.

Let every heart a song release,
In harmony with the divine.
Where worries cease, we find our peace,
In serenity, our souls entwine.

Echoes of Eternity in Quiet Spaces

In quietude, the spirit calls,
Echoes dance on gentle breeze.
Among the shadows, wisdom falls,
In whispered thoughts, the heart finds ease.

With every breath, the sacred flows,
Through valleys deep, and mountains high.
In time's embrace, the moment grows,
Infinity within the sigh.

As sacred seasons softly turn,
We gather light like autumn's gold.
In every flame, the fires burn,
A tapestry of stories told.

These quiet spaces hold our dreams,
An altar set for hearts to meet.
In still reflection, love redeems,
The echoes weave a world complete.

Seek solace in the silent night,
Where stars align with purpose clear.
In every echo, find the light,
And feel the vastness drawing near.

Soft Steps on Holy Ground

With humbled hearts, we tread in grace,
Upon this path of sacred love.
Each step a prayer and soft embrace,
Heaven beckons from above.

In holy whispers, truth unfolds,
As time stands still and hope reborn.
In every tale that faith upholds,
We find the light of every morn.

The earth beneath, a gentle guide,
With every breath, the spirit sings.
In harmony, we walk beside,
The angels' flight on healing wings.

Let laughter dance and sorrows fade,
As joy pervades the space we share.
In unity, our fears arrayed,
Soft steps on ground where love lays bare.

Together, hearts align as one,
In every moment, sacred sound.
We rise as children of the sun,
With faith profound on holy ground.

The Peace of Unfathomable Depths

In oceans deep, the spirit stirs,
Where silence speaks and wonders flow.
With every wave, His presence blurs,
In tranquil depths, we come to know.

A quiet stillness fills the air,
As hearts release their ancient sighs.
Within the calm, we shed despair,
And rise anew like morning skies.

Through every trial, love's embrace,
Guides us through storms that dare to rise.
In faith, we journey, seek His grace,
Unfathomable, like boundless skies.

The waters whisper, gentle truths,
As ripples weave our stories told.
In every heart, the hope renews,
A peace that never can grow cold.

Beyond the horizon, we can trust,
In depths profound, our spirits blend.
As anchored souls, we find our just,
In peace that flows, our journey's end.

The Divine Embrace of Silence

In silence, a sacred hush,
We find the peace we crave.
Whispers of the heart's soft touch,
God's presence in the wave.

Every breath, a gentle prayer,
In stillness, we belong.
The soul laid bare, beyond compare,
In silence, we grow strong.

Veils of noise, now torn apart,
Within, the truth will rise.
Each moment, a sacred art,
In stillness, hear the skies.

Beyond the chaos of the day,
Divine love does reside.
In silence, we will find our way,
With faith as our guide.

Let not the world's weight bring despair,
For we are held so close.
In sacred silence, we will share,
The grace that we love most.

Beneath the Veil of Whispered Grace

Beneath the veil, whispers sweet,
God's love like morning dew.
In quiet moments, souls do meet,
With every breath, it's true.

In the stillness, hearts unite,
Connected, yet apart.
Under stars, in soft twilight,
A dance within the heart.

Grace enfolds where shadows dwell,
In silence, darkness fades.
Each gentle word, a sacred spell,
In love, our fear cascades.

A hush that carries hope's sweet tune,
From lips to sky above.
In dusk's embrace and rising moon,
We surrender to His love.

So gather close, let silence speak,
In whispers, find your way.
With faith, the humble heart will seek,
The light of every day.

Hushed Offerings at Dawn's Break

At dawn's break, a quiet plea,
In hush, the world awakes.
With every breath, we come to see,
The path that love makes.

Each offering, a whispered prayer,
In light, we find our place.
Grateful hearts, in gentle care,
Hold on to divine grace.

Through the haze, the spirit soars,
With faith's soft, guiding hand.
Love opens kinder, brighter doors,
In silence, we shall stand.

In the colors of the morn,
Hope dances in the sky.
From the dark, we are reborn,
In faith, we learn to fly.

Let us gather, hearts aligned,
In quietude, take flight.
Hushed offerings to love defined,
Shall lead us to the light.

The Still Waters of Faith

By still waters, peace is found,
In reflection, souls do see.
A tranquil heart, a sacred ground,
Where love flows endlessly.

In the ripples, whispers call,
Trust the journey ahead.
In faith, we rise, and never fall,
For grace, like water, spreads.

Each moment, a chance to feel,
The depth of love within.
In stillness, hearts begin to heal,
Forgiveness for our sin.

As dawn breaks clear upon the shore,
Hope glimmers in the light.
With every wave, we find the more,
In faith, our spirits bright.

Let the waters guide your way,
With ease, we'll brave the tides.
In faith, our hearts forever sing,
With love that never hides.

Sacred Moments Wrapped in Stillness

In the hush of dawn's embrace,
Whispers of grace touch the soul.
Every heartbeat sings of faith,
In silence, we find our whole.

Moments wrapped in tender light,
The spirit dances, free and pure.
With each breath, a sacred gift,
In stillness, our hearts endure.

Gentle winds carry our prayers,
As we walk on paths unseen.
Through every tear and joyful laugh,
God's love flows like a stream.

In the quiet of the night,
Angels watch with loving eyes.
They guide us through the darkened fears,
Turning darkness into skies.

In this sacred space we meet,
The heart knows where to go.
Wrapped in love's eternal arms,
We bask in the gentle glow.

The Tranquil Path to Glory

On paths of peace, we wander slow,
With each step, the spirit grows.
Faith will be our guiding star,
Leading us to love's sweet home.

In the stillness, hear the song,
A melody of hope and grace.
With whispered prayers, we carry on,
United in this holy space.

Every moment ground in trust,
As faith lights our humble way.
In the shadows, we find strength,
Together we will not stray.

Radiance shines through the storm,
With patience, we shall abide.
Each burden shared will lighten hearts,
As love becomes our guide.

With open hearts, we lift our voices,
In harmony, we rise and sing.
The tranquil path unfolds before,
And in truth, we find our wings.

Illuminated by Inner Silence

In the stillness of the soul,
Truth reveals what lies within.
Hearts awakened, spirits whole,
In silence, we begin again.

A sacred flame ignites our core,
With whispers soft as morning dew.
Illuminated by the light,
The hidden paths unveil the new.

Through tranquil waters, we shall glide,
Every ripple speaks of grace.
In deep reflection, love abides,
With every gaze, the peace we chase.

The echoes of divine embrace,
Soft shadows dance and intertwine.
Here in silence, hearts find rest,
Illumined by a love divine.

So let the quiet hold us close,
In sacred stillness, we arise.
With hearts aligned to heaven's grace,
The spirit soars, the soul complies.

The Still Waters of Promise

By still waters, hope flows free,
A promise written in the sky.
With hearts open, we shall see,
The love that never says goodbye.

In the calm, the world dissolves,
Mirrored dreams reflect our prayer.
Every sigh a soft resolve,
Every heartbeat, love laid bare.

Flowing gently, grace abounds,
In stillness, we find our peace.
With gentle waves, our fear unwound,
In unity, our burdens cease.

As twilight beckons, shadows fade,
We gather in the fading light.
With every promise gently made,
The still waters keep us tight.

Beneath the stars, we lift our gaze,
With faith, we chart our course anew.
In the stillness of these days,
Guided by love, our dreams come true.

Prayers Woven in the Fabric of Silence

In silence deep, our hearts do call,
Whispers rise, a gentle thrall.
Threads of hope, in quiet spun,
Together we weave, 'til day is done.

Each prayer a stitch, a guiding light,
Binding souls in the holy night.
In every pause, a sacred breath,
A tapestry wrought of life and death.

Fingers trace the paths of grace,
In every silence, we seek His face.
Woven dreams on fabric fine,
Hearts entwined, in love divine.

As stillness reigns, our spirit's climb,
Echoes of peace transcend all time.
In the loom of faith, we find our way,
Prayers soft as dawn's first ray.

So let us gather, in hushed refrain,
Under the weight of joy and pain.
Through silent threads, our fates align,
Each whispered prayer, a sacred sign.

The Echoes of Faith in Hushed Realms

In the stillness, faith takes flight,
Echoes linger in the night.
Hearts attuned to whispers low,
In hushed realms, our spirits grow.

Softly spoken, truths unfold,
Stories of grace, quietly told.
In every shadow, light will break,
For faith's reverberance, we awake.

Through silence vast, the soul will soar,
In each heartbeat, we seek for more.
Guided by stars that shine above,
In the quiet, we touch His love.

The winds carry prayers on their wings,
Softly the hymn of hope that sings.
In tranquil spaces, peace we find,
Echoes of faith, beautifully aligned.

So come, let us dwell in this grace,
In the silence, our souls embrace.
In the echoes, our prayers are sealed,
In hushed realms, our fate revealed.

Divine Meditations in the Sacred Void

In the void, divine whispers call,
A sacred space where hearts enthrall.
Meditations rise like incense smoke,
In the silence, eternal hope.

Breath by breath, the spirit unites,
In the stillness, we scale great heights.
Calm waters reflect the sky,
In the sacred void, we learn to fly.

With open hearts, we seek and find,
Through the shadows, the light is kind.
Each moment, a treasure we hold,
In divine silence, stories told.

Listen closely, the pulse of grace,
In the void, we find our place.
Every heartbeat, a sacred song,
In this silence, we all belong.

Through meditations, the soul's ascent,
As we ponder life's great intent.
In the depths of the quiet, truth unfolds,
In sacred voids, love never grows old.

The Grace of a Silent Heart

In quiet corners, the heart does bloom,
A silent grace dispels all gloom.
With every heartbeat, love does start,
Finding refuge in a silent heart.

Soft as whispers, divine and true,
In silence, strength begins anew.
Each tender thought a work of art,
Bringing peace to the silent heart.

A balm for wounds, in stillness found,
In quietude, our souls unbound.
With loving kindness, we impart,
The simple grace of a silent heart.

As we gather in tranquil places,
Grace illuminates, and fear displaces.
In the calm, our burdens part,
Revealing the power of a silent heart.

Embrace the quiet, let worries cease,
In stillness, we discover peace.
In every breath, a holy chart,
To navigate with a silent heart.

A Refuge of Serenity in the Storm

In tempest's grip, we seek Your hand,
A shelter found in holy land.
Amidst the roar, our hearts remain,
In faith we rise, transcending pain.

Your whispers calm the raging sea,
With every breath, You set us free.
In winds that howl, we hear Your voice,
In trust we stand, in hope rejoice.

The storm may rage, but we are still,
Your presence graces all we will.
In shadows deep, Your love will guide,
We find our peace, where fears subside.

Through trials faced, we hold so tight,
We linger in Your sacred light.
Our refuge strong, our hearts align,
In every struggle, we are Thine.

As storms may pass and skies may clear,
We gather strength, our souls draw near.
In sanctuary of Your grace,
A refuge found in love's embrace.

The Breath of God in Muffled Time

In quiet moments, stillness blooms,
A sacred hush where love consumes.
With every beat, we call Your name,
Your breath ignites the heart's own flame.

In shadows cast by fleeting hours,
You drape our lives with holy flowers.
In muffled time, our souls align,
With whispers soft, divinely fine.

The heart's reflection, soft and clear,
In trust we dwell, with You so near.
As silence weaves its gentle lace,
We find our strength in Your embrace.

Each heartbeat echoes love profound,
In every sigh, Your grace is found.
In every pause, we sense the dive,
The Breath of God, we are alive.

Through muted days, Your light will shine,
Awakening spirits, truly divine.
In time's embrace, we stand as one,
With faith revived, our journey's begun.

The Unseen Light of Prayerful Reflections

In sacred thoughts, our spirits soar,
Beyond the veil, we seek, implore.
Within the silence, wisdom dwells,
In whispered truths, Your love compels.

The unseen light that guides our way,
In prayerful moments, night and day.
With each reflection, grace unfolds,
In quiet trust, our hearts are bold.

Through trials faced, we lift our gaze,
In faith we journey through the maze.
With every prayer, our burdens laid,
The unseen light will never fade.

As echoes fade, Your voice remains,
In love's embrace, we break our chains.
Each thought a prayer, each deed a chance,
To stand in light, to find our dance.

In moments still, where hope ignites,
We find the truth within the nights.
The unseen light, our guiding star,
In prayerful hearts, we know who we are.

Grace Unfolds in Silent Communion

In silent halls, where shadows blend,
Our hearts converge, our souls ascend.
With every breath, a prayer we weave,
In grace unfurled, we now believe.

The whispered calm, profound and deep,
In solitude, our spirits leap.
With open hands, we seek to find,
The grace that flows through heart and mind.

As silence wraps us in its shroud,
We find our strength within the loud.
In sacred space, where time stands still,
We drink from love, we seek Your will.

In every sigh, Your presence near,
We find the light that casts out fear.
In communion pure, our hearts entwine,
In grace revealed, Your love is mine.

Through quiet moments, trust expands,
We lift our voices, join our hands.
In silent grace, our spirits fuse,
In sacred love, we gently choose.

A Prayer Amidst the Leaves

O gentle rustle, hear my pleas,
In the embrace of ancient trees.
Silent echoes, sacred air,
Whispered hopes, a humble prayer.

Sunlight dances through the boughs,
Kneeling softly, I make my vows.
Nature's hymn, a guiding star,
In this moment, near and far.

Swaying branches, souls unite,
In the calm of morning light.
With each leaf that falls to ground,
I find solace, peace profound.

O Lord of nature, hear my song,
In every heart, where we belong.
As seasons change, my spirit seeks,
In the calmness, my soul speaks.

Let your love, like roots, grow deep,
In every flower, every leap.
Through the leaves, my heart does soar,
In your goodness, I find more.

The Solace of Divine Whisper

Amidst the noise, a quiet sound,
In sacred silence, I am found.
Divine whispers, soft and clear,
Calling me, drawing me near.

In shadowed corners, peace does dwell,
A gentle voice where sorrows quell.
Each trembling leaf, a soft embrace,
In this space, I seek Your grace.

The world may rage, yet I stand still,
In the echo, I find Your will.
Through trials faced, Your love remains,
In whispered words, my heart gains.

O Sacred Spirit, guide my way,
Through dusk and dawn, come what may.
In every heartbeat, Your wisdom flows,
A timeless truth, deep within grows.

Beneath the stars, together we roam,
In sacred whispers, I find my home.
With every breath, I speak Your name,
In this journey, I feel the same.

Where Profound Meets Profound

In the stillness of the sacred night,
Where shadows dance, and hearts take flight.
I seek Your face, in moonlit grace,
In this moment, I find my place.

Wisdom flows like rivers wide,
As the universe becomes my guide.
In the silence, thoughts intertwine,
Where depth meets depth, the soul aligns.

Here in still waters, reflections gleam,
A tapestry woven, thread of dream.
In every heartbeat, questions arise,
Where profound truths fill the skies.

O Infinite Spirit, shine Your light,
On paths unseen, through dark and bright.
In this journey, hand in hand,
Together we walk, together we stand.

With each reverberation, truth we seek,
In love's embrace, we find the weak.
As stars in chorus, our spirits sing,
In every heartbeat, the joy You bring.

A Sanctuary of Unheard Melodies

In the quietude of morning's grace,
I find Your love, a warm embrace.
Whispers linger, soft and sweet,
In the sanctuary where hearts meet.

Each note of silence tells a tale,
In hidden realms where souls prevail.
In depths of heart, melodies flow,
Guiding me where I must go.

In colors bright that paint the sky,
I hear the laughter as time slips by.
Every hue, a soft refrain,
A symphony beyond the rain.

O Divine Maestro, lead me on,
Through every dusk until the dawn.
In this realm of unheard songs,
I find strength, where love belongs.

As shadows dance and twilight glows,
In unseen places, Your spirit flows.
In harmony, I find my place,
In the sanctuary of Your grace.

A Pilgrimage Toward Inner Tranquility

In silence, we tread the sacred path,
Seeking solace among the hills.
With every step, burdens release,
The heart opens to quiet thrills.

The stream flows gently by our side,
Whispering secrets of the ground.
Each breath a prayer, each gaze a gift,
In nature's arms, our peace is found.

Under the vast and starry skies,
We lay our thoughts to rest at night.
The universe hums a soft tune,
Guiding us toward the purest light.

In moments still, we hear the call,
A voice of love, so deep, profound.
Embracing grace in every fall,
A pilgrimage where souls abound.

With hearts aligned to love's embrace,
We walk together, hand in hand.
Each dawn, a chance to seek and find,
The beauty of the promised land.

Divine Harmony in the Heart of Stillness

In stillness, time begins to slow,
The whispers of the soul arise.
In sacred breath, our spirits grow,
A melody where the heart lies.

As dawn stretches its golden rays,
We find our place, serene, awake.
In nature's choir, we join the praise,
Surrendering to the peace we take.

The rustling leaves, a sign from above,
Each moment speaks of grace divine.
In silence, we feel the push of love,
A harmony, a sacred sign.

Amid the chaos of the day,
The stillness beckons us to pause.
In quietude, we find our way,
In every breath, a sacred cause.

Awakening to life anew,
Our hearts unite in gentle prayer.
In divine calm, we find the view,
The essence of love everywhere.

Echoes of Creation in Gentle Whispers

In the hush, the world unfolds,
Soft echoes of creation's song.
Nature's breath, in tales retold,
In every shadow, we belong.

With each rustle, whispers dance,
The beauty found in each embrace.
Life's sacred threads weave cosmic chance,
Connecting us in time and space.

The winds carry tales of the past,
In songbirds' calls, we hear the choir.
In every heartbeat, shadows cast,
The sacred fire guiding higher.

In hidden corners of the heart,
The echoes linger, soft and true.
From solitude, we can depart,
To find the light of me and you.

So let us listen to the flow,
To nature's pulse, a gentle sound.
In whispers of divine, we grow,
In every moment, we are found.

The Soul's Song in Sacred Retreat

In sacred spaces, we unwind,
The soul's song sings of inner peace.
In stillness, love is redefined,
Each moment whispers sweet release.

Beneath the trees, we close our eyes,
In nature's arms, confusion fades.
The heart awakens, quiet sighs,
In solitude, the spirit wades.

The water's edge reflects our dreams,
Rippling softly in the light.
Each drop a story, as it seems,
A journey shared by day and night.

With every breath, the world dissolves,
In this retreat, we find our space.
Embracing all, our heart evolves,
In love's embrace, we seek His grace.

Through valleys deep, through mountains high,
The soul's song guides our humble way.
With faith, we learn to soar and fly,
In sacred retreat, forever stay.

The Lord's Voice in the Quietude

In stillness, His whispers flow,
A gentle breeze, a soft glow.
He speaks in shadows, grace revealed,
In silent moments, hearts are healed.

The rustle of leaves tells His tale,
A comforting hand, not faint nor pale.
Each heartbeat echoes wisdom so pure,
In solitude, His love is sure.

With every breath, His presence near,
A guiding star, a soul's sincere.
Through valleys low and mountains high,
He leads us gently, by and by.

When burdens weigh and trials surge,
In quiet prayer, our spirits merge.
The Lord's voice, like a soothing balm,
In the chaos, we find our calm.

So listen closely to the night,
In darkness, He is our light.
The Lord's voice sings within our soul,
In quietude, we are made whole.

Serenity: A Celestial Covenant

In the twilight's calm embrace,
He promises peace, a holy space.
A tranquil heart, a whispered vow,
In faith, He thrives, here and now.

Each star that twinkles in the night,
Is a testament of His light.
A covenant that we hold dear,
In the silence, He draws near.

With every dawn, His mercies new,
In every prayer, a love so true.
He washes sorrow from our tears,
In serenity, quelling fears.

The winds of grace through branches sway,
In nature's choir, we choose to pray.
Together we rise, united in love,
Guided by Him, the One above.

So let our hearts in stillness bloom,
In the sacred space, dispel the gloom.
A celestial promise, forever we share,
In serenity, we find our prayer.

Celestial Calm in the Heart of Prayer

In the stillest hour, His spirit beams,
A refuge found, in sacred dreams.
The heart whispers of faith profound,
In the quiet, His grace abounds.

As clouds retreat, the heavens sigh,
In every moment, we lift our cry.
The calm descends, like morning mist,
In prayer, our souls find bliss.

With every breath, a sacred space,
In seeking Him, we know His grace.
Celestial calm, a balm divine,
In every thought, His peace we find.

The echoes of love in silence ring,
As angels gather, voices sing.
In unified hearts, our spirits soar,
In prayer's embrace, forevermore.

So let us kneel and seek His face,
In reverent hush, we find our place.
The celestial calm, a holy sign,
In the heart of prayer, we intertwine.

Light Breaking Through the Quiet Gloom

In shadows deep, His light breaks through,
A guiding hand, a promise true.
When sorrow lingers, hope appears,
His radiant love dispels our fears.

With each dawn, a new rebirth,
In sacred silence, we know our worth.
The gloom recedes, as daylight streams,
By faith ignited, we chase our dreams.

In weathered hearts, the spirit glows,
Beneath the weight, His mercy flows.
Each tear we shed becomes a spark,
Transforming pain to joy from dark.

So lift your eyes to skies above,
In the quiet, embrace His love.
The light that shines, unyielding, bright,
Guides us through the deepest night.

In every struggle, every strain,
His radiant presence eases pain.
Light breaking through, so warm, so sweet,
In quiet gloom, we stand complete.

Milton Keynes UK
Ingram Content Group UK Ltd.
UKHW020044271124
451585UK00012B/1038